# FROM ME TO YOU PT.2
# KING'S WAVE

## JOEL WASHINGTON ATTERBERRY

From Me to You Pt. 2 King's Wave

Copyrighted © 2021 Library of Congress

Published by Joel Washington Atterberry

ISBN: 9781735295244


Contact Information

Email: kingatterberry7@gmail.com

Facebook: Joel Washington Atterberry

Instagram: king_atterberry7

Instagram: mentallity9

Editor: Julia C Dozier

Illustration by Charm Hallingquest

# Mindful Thoughts

Enjoying the fact that in our everyday lives, we experience feelings and emotions.
So, I say bring a smile upon the women of today, whether it is a look, or a kind word expression.
I would like to think my mannerism reflects the gentleman that I am, existing in this world.
There are still more things to figure out, understand and comprehend.

# Table of Contents

# Flashing!

Outside the walls of your interior made up from your energy.

Love you immensely feel like god sent you to me.

Hold on to your story with compassion and care.

What you have given me is what I gave

back rare.

Songs that I love so much reaching my core and all.

Dreaming about your fine self therefore I pour.

The way that I feel letting it spill until it fills.

Compartments inside your physical you know the deal.

Misters talk that, until we have a one on one.

Plan it out and have fun so time is satisfaction.

Spiritually I see you and know from higher powers.

That I want to encounter an experience here is your flowers.

## Flashing! Pt.2

Can I explore an opportunity to join you for one night?

Until your heart changes its feeling, and I am always in your sight.

Write you powerful poems and recite them 'til you are stuffed.

Your ears had enough, and you allow my hands to touch.

Be myself and caress your skin that look so soft and lovely.

With my magical powers I would love to visually study.

You are a natural so fascinating upon my open eyes.

Have us disappear into a galaxy by flying high.

Kiss your lips while holding your hands very nicely.

The feeling is a quenched sensation like drinking iced tea.

Embrace inside a beautiful hug that move reality.

Turning into a fantasy I hear only you call to me.

Under familiarity as if as we been here before.

If this did really occur, please keep it safely stored.

Cannot even express although I am trying my damn best.

This what I get off my chest while I am writing for the best.

## Skeleton key

How are you feeling, Love? How was your day? What are you doing?

I know you just got home from work and probably cooling.

After your relaxing, chilling and unwinding.

Give me a call while you are hiding and sighing.

Place your time back in the world I know it is hard.

Become a superstar and beat out the odds.

You're sweet and lovely let us rock how we should be.

Do not leave me in the cold because your ex carry jealousy.

You know what it is let us talk laugh and chill.

No rush on my behalf I am just keeping it real.

Sometime in life we must go for what we know.

Enjoy what's special release what is stressful.

My monetary moments carry sandman properties.

Forget Mother Nature, Father Time cannot stop me.

A wave in the water that be touching the sand.

Real life story of the man behind the hands.

Allow my voice to enter where all the others failed.

Take you on a journey let nature prevail.

Can I bring you a memory of something A+?

We do not have to be low key if it is just us.

**Have you seen her!**

Inside my all-star inquiries my modesty
is honesty.

Getting to know you better is a
universal quality.

Speaking the living words that reside
within the unknown.

This appreciated poem can be held
inside your hearts home.

When I look into your eyes beside
seeing your pretty smile.

Although it is occasionally but I am
digging your whole style.

Keep me in your thoughts of thought,
do not ever let it sever.

As time move about, I stamp your
moments in my letters.

Capture your beautiful visual it
enhances how I get lyrical.

As if I just meditated to a smooth jazz instrumental.

The warm words that I embrace off the lips on your face.

I have gotten to know so well that I would not mind tasting.

Reminding me of a story of a couple that love the seventies.

Living off the hope and drive of seeing one's destiny.

So, my scenes in dreams written through composition notes.

It is no joke when you awoke seeing both sides of growth.

New cord plug it in!

Recalibration done created off vibration.

Extension visiting planes in dimensions.

Listening to sounds that carry high frequency.

Waves enter me causing reflection of memory.

Center piece active slow to what just happened.

No idea grabbing just safe peaceful rapping.

Trajectory points measured aligned with living.

Let it go whatever is missing build a bridge in your kitchen.

Cook a different type of grub or prep a verbal sub.

Secret ingredients are flavor mixed with style and love.

Cadence to the street speak with different heat.

Forget whoever is deep fix the ground of thee elite.

Better surface than the earth is yet do not make them nervous.

Alleviate the service of purpose and check the furthest.

Cause all it takes is one time to send out the beacon.

Around the corner is the wave that will have the people speaking.

# First love

The one who had me open is the same one I had open.

Times that we were floating our wings almost got broken.

Route that we had chosen was a path that we had taken.

So involved with one another that her family approved our dating.

Catching the train to the Bronx from Harlem one two five.

Talking and joking around as we sat side to side.

As a young dude she called the house to make sure that I am home.

Before her trip to where I lived so we can get in our zone.

Walking around the certain parts of New York City.

Whether the hot Summer days or the Winter when it was chilly.

She was Dominican spoke without conversation hidden.

Making sure I would listen while she spoke and start grinning.

Initiating arguments just to see what would happen.

I started laughing and gave a look, kissed her lips with passion.

Discussing moments with no trust that is what ended us.

We had the natural chemistry, but it just was not enough.

So, we telephoned goodbyes and went about our separate ways.

For two and a half years of niceness I moved away.

Never to look back started life on a different track.

But still my thoughts were blank on a situation way back.

Although you never know what life have has in store for you to view.

I am just sharing a short story a first love I once knew.

**Let us go until we get there!**

This one night that we both share,

undress each other with a fair stare.

Moment in time our fears and care

bring a daydream out of nowhere.

No consequences on the back board

you know exactly what we came for.

Natural occurrence of a nice afternoon

or a midnight

cruise in closed doors.

Hug the love with a tasteful embrace,

time is lost on our mental escape.

Heart race let me slow it down for you,

all that matter is a memorable date.

Eyes closed feel the vibes and
connect,

sweet kisses on your cheek and neck.

Mutual respect on what comes next,

let me show how the real KING get.

Passionate touches on your arms and breast

slide hands on hips and thighs.

It's becoming warm outside of our norm,

enjoy the nice friendly skies.

## Let's go until we get there! V2

Cloud nine feeling is the atmosphere.

shift gears as we preserve.

From far to near love can be sincere

there's no need to get prepared.

Flavor new as I'm having you,

continue do what your heart want to.

Reach our destination when our bodies
in-tune,

I am glad you chose to come through.

Beautiful soul that you are to me,

call me anytime just to release.

You are my candy girl in this whole
damn world,

I hope you found peace in me.

Bring my words to life around your soul
when I speak,

this is all that I built for you.

The lines that I say in and out of the bed,

right now, baby girl I showed and proved.

Cannot wait till we have other times to chill,

explore policies on the door.

This moment so balanced within our own challenge,

purification rich and raw.

# I got your back!

If you want to know just in case that you forgot.

You are the one and only flavor that always hit the spot.

When I feel the need to inhale the air you breathe.

You are the seventh sea that I would sail out to see.

Even get lost without direction but use a mental compass.

Utilize my knowledge of self to keep a promise.

Formulate a plan to always be honest please believe.

This is a king atterberry message worn on my sleeves.

Allow me to give you my heart, mind and soul.

Even speak to me mentioning my name as joel.

So, in love with being around you that I miss you so much.

It has been a long-time face to face remind me what is up.

## Nothing less

All the fun times we had under the polluted air was strong.

Wish we could have them moments again in a higher spiritual form.

Just to look into your eyes face to face and smell your fragrance.

These are my thoughts put down on paper because you are my favorite.

Beautiful woman that you are so heavenly seen by my heart.

Gotta be honest to me you set the bar high with a mark.

It is cool for how it be and that is between you and me.

I speak with god before I sleep to answer prayers on my belief.

Society has been bitten with a pandemic issue.

Wrote this poem because I miss you although on screens, I see you.

So, the time you make for me I appreciate and love it.

The justice of being trusted is like a blessing in abundance.

When your worries are on the table rest your feeling on your friend.

I am always open for conversation whenever you wanna begin.

Morning moon or night hit me up and I will be there.

One thing that we both share love for each other that is rare.

# The wave

Meet the henny king doing anything to enter daydreams.

Brighten up a scene with a glass of wine for a sweet thing.

My choice is white instead of red enjoy your Merlot.

I came to let you know how I am after my show.

Place thoughts on paragraphs with an III twelve liner.

Go deeper than a diver break walls like a coal miner.

When I find something no hunting, I come across it.

Become smooth as Billy dee Williams or Richard Lawson.

Will you be my lady not singing the blues on course?

Invitation to the shore and explore the water for sure.

Absorb the ambiance of nature when I take you.

I am not trying to snake you or fake you I am grateful.

To have you visit and have a great time that is exquisite.

Just know that king atterberry is all about his business.

Inject your mind with memories of having a nice time.

Because when I shine you shine it is fresher than winter pines.

**Today is your tomorrow, tomorrow is today!**

**Happy is the man that fall in love with a woman of truth.**

**What else is there to do when you admire someone beautiful.**

**Smile so heavenly this must be what god has for me.**

**Wondering about this lovely image created full of energy.**

**My night and day of thinking if she opens to take a chance.**

**Feeling so joyful at the thought of having a verbal dance.**

**Which could lead to special times of getting to know one another.**

**Allow my spirit to touch her and protect her auras colors.**

**Display my sense of humor if I can be myself.**

Take the chill away provide a way to make her heart melt.

Speaking life into existence whether near far or distant.

Be persistent with commitment as she speaks about ambition.

Queen oh my god you trigger emotions in my physical.

Let's have a maybe probably party so I can get close to you.

I am man who is caring and compassionate on breathing.

And I'm ok if you are leading when I'm treating on our greeting.

# Finding fresh focus!!

Left the concrete jungle found a
working hustle.

Many years at the shore built up a lot
of muscle.

Some of the woman I cuddle they love
the man that is gentle.

Past time lovers be mental hoping the
king rekindle.

Searching out for the real queen we
start off as cordial.

Maybe one day be loyal if you see me, I
saw you.

Touch your thoughts if it is right there
it is almost end of years.

In my head I am like oh yeah baby girl
makes it real clear.

I will drop whatever you want to be
secure in the core.

King knocking at the doors let me know about the tour.

Exploring some possibilities walk through life with humility.

Ills of the world are killing me need a love that consider me.

The type they like who excite the world they live in.

Making time by chilling also playing the right position.

If a ghost is your host and the approach is not close.

Send out a call through the morning while he drinks his coffee roast.

# Brown sugar love jones

Thought it was you and I just forget the other guy.

Allow my eyes to look inside while your heart is open wide.

Provide you with mystery and replay our history.

Remember kissing me as I caressed your body.

Touch on moments where there were no dark days.

All the times you were afraid I moved them all away.

While your smile was kept beautiful instead of miserable.

As we walked around, I saw different men hitting on you.

Only by a stare and a look I moved you closer.

When your girlfriends had you doubt me, I rebuilt my motor.

Ran with an exquisite living purpose of being.

Brought to life your dreams yet they had you scheming.

So, I turned into a soldier of love and found another.

Who could open a window and look inside her lover?

No longer on standby I rise like no other, bye!

Wipe the tears from your eyes we gave it a good try.

To be so in love with you and always so comfortable.

Amazing and wonderful that you allowed me to know you.

Our worlds are so personal cannot ever stop thinking bout.

The times I am in the house on my couch Inside a drought.

So, I pray maybe one day you receive my special May Day.

Send a signal to the shore I reside in north cape May.

Waiting for that beacon of light to shine upon me.

Meet you at a destination with my lovely angel army.

Music and love are so well placed together.

As if affection and intimacy bring forth sunny weather.

Good vibes and prosperity of existing in great moments.

This is my open letter written by me the chosen poet.

# Pardon me! (Story of LO)

Must be some other shit that is why she must be over kid.

Dipped out the sour mix checking all his fingerprints.

Once never too busy but now question who he is.

Who is she that is supposed to be his one and only?

The access to enter do not linger its fair exchange.

On a month, his mother's pain transformed to cold rain.

As he celebrates her born day feelings upon his mourning.

Waking up late afternoon from sleeping through the morning.

Only one that held him closely deep into his heart.

Is the love carrying women that refuse to throw darts?

As he tries to find work masking the hurt and disappointment.

Soon hope to be taking on a position for employment.

Gutter way was typical but had to grab some different views.

Or end up on the news looking mad with a lot of fools.

Street life is not the same as before tried to explain.

Too many others and society he blames for his change.

Made a call to a person with contacts hoping he fall back.

Get him back on track so he removes what hold him back.

Upon belief at many time gotta start at the bottom.

Then elevate to a level where you good
and not starving.

Love can be shown from afar embrace
the friendship.

Lost in the sentence remember this
from the member sent.

## Only for you

Can I play with your words inside the lines to express mine?

As my clock stands still touch any hand that gives you time.

Place my seconds on your minutes and wonder about an hour.

Few moments of taking it all in see if we have power.

Look into your eyes allow my vibes to send a blend.

Of comfortable sensations that attract your attention.

Hold the highest points of memory while absorbing your energy.

Keeping my mind free as I dream about you kissing me.

Paris in my mind as the French become our pinch.

---

Co-exist within a rift or in a drift that make sense.

Draw your image to my thoughts while I remain on course.

Listening to your voice as I fall for you at any cost.

## KING'S PARTIAL WAVE

The Inner side of me is an external part
of my journey.
Walking through the smoke, screen and
mirrors that's paranormal.
Embedded within my sight is a hidden
emotion of darkness.
Cold enough to stop motion and give
love to those heartless.
Never mind my image it's been
sentenced with a resemblance.
Trapped in a deliverance of clearance
minding my business.
Leave me be, go about your own way
so I can face fate.
My spirit haven't located the face of
faith in my stone state.

When I'm visible and fresh out of my
undisturbed rest.
Keeping my half mane framed top of
my head is blessed.
Walk away don't test on what's slept
I'm only searching.
For unanswered questions that been
emerging from those hurting.

# Best of the best

All the fun times we had under the
polluted air was strong.
Wish we could have them moments
again in a universal form.
Just to look into your eyes face to face
and smell your fragrance.
My thoughts put down on paper
because you are my favorite.
Beautiful woman that you are that is
seen by my heart.
Gotta be honest to me you made a
mark inside a spark.
It is cool for how it be and that is
between you and me.
I speak with god before I sleep to
answer prayers on my belief.

Society has been bitten with a
pandemic issue.
Wrote this poem because I miss you
although on screens, I see you.
So, the time you make for me I
appreciate and love it.
The justice of being trusted is like a
blessing in abundance.
When your worries are on the table rest
your feeling on your friend.
I am always open for conversation
whenever you wanna begin.
Morning moon or night hit me up and I
will be there.
One thing that we both share love for
each other that is rare.

## Paper wings!

Allow the ink to hit the page I am already on my way.

Checking for better days there is no time to play.

Surfing upon the wave I am grounded and balanced.

Exploiting my talent, it is apparent how I can manage.

Note pad on deck much respect to my pen game.

Mindset is insane it is hard for me to explain.

Flyer and higher than my conscious on material.

Check whatever is due my new groove is imperial.

King is my name royalty is in my veins.

Move about with Phoenix wings that carry a certain flame.

Internal fire burning the fuel is natural energy.

Cannot destroy my character are you really kidding me.

Resonate with properties captured from outer earth.

Visit another galaxy that showed off my worth.

Transported back through a portal that is formal.

Through my eyes from the sky opened the ones who saw you.

**Mirror my soul!**

**Which side of me get you, tell me what side is special?**

**I wanna know how to catch you because you do not settle.**

**Broadband my signals that is what I be into.**

**Mystical and magical auras that are essential.**

**Ancestral prayers upon forming words that is heard.**

**Sweeter than songbirds giving birth sounds purged.**

**Lift my spirit sky high till I see heavens magnificent.**

**Radiant beautiful formation that looks extravagant.**

Transport myself through stillness wake up brilliant.

God knows I feel privileged feeling his glory in it.

Dive inside the realm of music tuning my mind.

Enjoying divine chimes which reminds me of a time.

Capture the moment when I was down and out of luck.

Now it is aww shucks giving an audience more than what.

Little bits of this which was missed so here I sit.

In a chair controlling patterns of breathing feel my kiss.

# Match to match

Entering rings trying to survive though they want me to take a dive.

Whether or not if I apply some of my thoughts I must divide.

In between the here and now sparring around within my style.

Expression presented loud imagery formed from out the clouds.

Who am I currently coming back to finish?

Reincarnated to visit and travel pass the limits.

Expose yourself to the higher expectation of who you are.

For I am like aww here you are the loveliest of them all.

No more chains on feet what better to
hold me.
Involve yourself around me my cipher
almost complete.
One eighty plus a ninety just been
waiting since the beginning.
What's trending never ending just
finding a place to blend in.
Hope saw no law judgment of emotions
door.
Guard your house of love find peace
with mi amore.
It is not hard figure out without asking
to know my passion.
Though I live in south jersey been
learned a lot in Manhattan.

## Black Movie Love

Best deeds about last night witness
Sylvie's love.
After waiting to exhale brown sugar I
miss you much.
After a love jones why did I get married
the best man condoned it.
Two can play the game hmm love and
basketball moment.
Allow me to let you connect to me
phenomenally successful.
Beyond the lights anything can be
pure, raw and special.
Medicine for melancholy drawing
disappearing acts.
I could be south side with you if god
have my back.

Keep that she wants a poetic justice
after thinking like a man.

Queen and slim plans with a just wright
program.

Check fences along the photograph of
Jason's lyric.

If Beale street could talk enjoying
Claudine's music.

## Black Movie Love Pt. 2

The perfect match may set up a
temptation premature.
Thin line between love and hate, shoot
a shot, with no score.
Enter a last holiday with a woman like
the preachers' wife.
Outside of the holy doors you may just
want to think twice.
catch a flick or a show whether it's
have or have not.
Do not get caught up in a hype leaving
you stuck in one spot.
Lost in boomerang do not play yourself
with a Carmen jones.
Find yourself with purple rain in
baggage claim all alone.

Commitments a film by carol Mayes is
still today.
The love letter from out the blue might
be on its way.
Under the cherry moon watching a
graffiti bridge.
Enjoy the art with who you with until
you find your niche!

# My hand for you

When that time come I am already on
display.
Don't let them others sway what you
are thinking okay.
No need to search for prayers or look
at windows open.
My motion be holding a different life
inside oceans.
Thoughts occur facing my visual scan
for love.
I know that you had it tough and you're
missing a royal touch.
The idea of what could be mix the
chemistry of me.
Better side of what's to be is a unity
living free.

No expectation congratulations you let
your guard down.
Found inside a king is a thrown with a
magnificent crown.
Mindful ideas as they appear kissing
your tears.
Inner peace aware hold your memories
like souvenirs.
Change into scuba gear travel against
the tides.
Escaping inside your high that your low
had to be neutralized.
And With you by my side I will let god
decide.
The biggest treasure to find is LOVE
without it compromised.
All natural without without being
forced believe in the source.

The thrill can bring a chill or a

happiness cough.

This is my soft letter written different

seen in your vision.

While we connect let's improvise on

this edition.

## Time before

Use to dream that I mastered many ways to capture.

Covered your whole rapture moved a little faster.

Couldn't fall short on the steps to get to know you.

Speaking to you on the phone was very soulful.

Conversation and laughter about many things.

Schedule a time to meet up how can we swing.

Perhaps maybe lunch or dinner your choice Is fine.

feel me inside of these lines it is divine.

Your glow is incredible angels get jealous.

just another side of god's creation treasured.

Maybe stay friendly going toward summer.

Only you and I sweet thing I'm not a runner.

Here's the real deal on why I wanna speak.

feeling your energy from another side of me.

If you are ok and feel the same as I.

Open the possibility for this cool guy.

Won't be disappointed though we never
know.

The name is atterberry first name is
joel.

**Special thanks:**

To all the good women that never judged me but allowed me to be myself.

And I enjoyed the many conversations about love inside relationships good and bad.

All books available on amazon!
Search under the titles.

*Through My Eyes from the Sky*
*Through My Eyes from the Sky, Part 2*
*Marvelous Measures of Me*
*Seeing the World Through My*
*Spiritual Eyes*
*From Me to You: The Memo".*
*January 2019*
*Just Like Candy: The Gallotron Files*
*The Gallotron Files, Part 2. Back on*
*Earth*
*The Man Behind the Hands*